"Sometimes all that ˏ
you read *Wild Girls*—a book that is golden. Brewer's sartorial
poems dazzle with language personalizing poems with humor
and pathos. The seduction and glamour of clothing often carries
the poet's themes—funny and sad, sweet and soulful— but
the extraordinary realization is that sensuality can define our
humanity. Each poem wears an unruined heart, the brightest
apparel of all."

—Grace Cavalieri, Maryland Poet Laureate

"'Color matters,' as do scents and textures, sights and sounds:
Shirley Brewer's *Wild Girls* is alive to the senses to an
extraordinary degree. What's not to love in a collection that so
effectively deploys fashion as objective correlative for the ups and
downs, the love, loss, and adventures richly lived by vivid women.
Like the 'feisty babes' who populate this book, Brewer's wise and
witty poems 'conjure magic spells [and] spark an abundance of
pluck.'"

—Moira Egan, *Amore e Morte*

"The poems in *Wild Girls* 'shoot the ashes off the end of a
cigarette.' Poet Shirley J. Brewer deftly pins both the well-known
and unsung heroines to the skies of her imagination. From Annie
Oakley to Queen Elizabeth II to Jackie Kennedy to Breonna
Taylor, she captivates the senses with a fragrant and richly-hued
assemblage rife with pain, joy, humor and grace. Brewer conjures a
thrilling magic in this important collection, triumphantly evoking
flashes of both Plath and Duhamel."

—Dean Bartoli Smith, *Baltimore Sons*

WILD GIRLS

Shirley J. Brewer

Apprentice
House Press
Loyola University Maryland

First Edition

Paperback ISBN: 978-1-62720-437-8
Ebook ISBN: 978-1-62720-438-5

Cover photo courtesy of NASA's Hubble Telescope www.hubblesite.org
Author photo by Bonnie Schupp

Design by Riley Kamm
Promotional plan by Rachel Brooks
Editorial Development by Sophie LaBella

Published by Apprentice House Press

Apprentice
House Press
Loyola University Maryland

Loyola University Maryland
4501 N. Charles Street, Baltimore, MD 21210
410.617.5265
www.ApprenticeHouse.com
info@ApprenticeHouse.com

In memory of
these beloved Wild Girls

Rezsin Adams
Frana Vermilyea Brown
Norma Chapman
Doris Dunker
Lee Lougée
Elaine McCarthy
Elizabeth McWethy
Frances Helen Brewer Nostrand
Patricia Owens
Bonnie Schupp
Kay Weinstein
Muriel Weinstein

Acknowledgments

Grateful acknowledgment is made to the editors of the following journals in which some of the poems first appeared, sometimes in slightly different forms:

Barrow Street, "Jackie"

Calyx, "Consolation"

Chiron Review, "Unveiled," "I Could've Been *The Godmother*, 1983," "To Job's Wife"

Comstock Review, "The Secret Life of Body Parts," "My Sister's Schizophrenia," "The History of Female Evolution: A Brief," "Yellow Anthem"

Edison Literary Review, "Where Did the Wild Girl Go," "Song of Lavender"

Evening Street Review, "Wild Bill's Wife"

Gargoyle, "Marilyn Speaks," "Annie O," "Queen Kong"

Glimpse Poetry Magazine, "Carnival Blossoms"

Innisfree Poetry Journal, "Noah's Wife"

Little Patuxent Review, "I Am Marilyn Monroe's Lipstick"

Loch Raven Review, "General Custer's Wife," "Glitz at the Musée," "Elegy for Sandra Bland," "Of Mice and Smoke," "The Cone Sisters," "Jezebel," "The Belle of Baltimore," "My Plain Romance"

Manorborn, "The Body Washer"

Naugatuck River Review, "Aunt Emma, On Forgiving the Cow," "Yum Yum Gardens," "The Sisterhood of the Troubling Parts"

New Verse News, "Boston Marathon, 2013"

Paterson Literary Review, "Spring Break," "Great Elixirs"

Plainsongs, "Let This Be the Place," "Mermaids in the Basement"

Poetica Review, "What the Terrorists Do Not See," "Beneath the Pomp of Circumstance"

Poetry East, "Marathon of Necessity," "What the Bride Wore," "I Shop with the Queen"

San Pedro River Review, "Only Trouble Is, Gee Whiz"

Slant, "Modern Torso of Apollo," "The Language of Hair," "Hope is the thing with salt and pepper shakers"

The Five-Two, "For the Love of Death"

The Potomac, "All of Us Wanted to Be Annette"

Welter, "Girl in a Pink Dress," "Charade," "Dinner Date with Richard Gere," "Lament for a Cowgirl"

"Consolation" was reprinted in the chapbook, *A Little Breast Music,* Passager Books, 2008, in which the following poem also appeared: "Alice in China"

"For His Maryfrances" was published in *Bluebird* magazine, Winter 2010-11, and also appeared in *life in me like grass on fire: love poems,* a Maryland Writers' Association anthology, 2011

"A Sugar Maple Tree on St. Paul Street," was published in the *Baltimore Post-Examiner,* 2013

"Alvina and the Bishop" appeared in *Poetry in Medicine,* an anthology published by Persea Books, 2015

"Highballs" appeared in *Bay to Ocean: The Year's Best Writing from the Eastern Shore,* an anthology published by the Eastern Shore Writers Association, 2019

Contents

I started out as a girl
without a shadow, in iron shoes;
now, at the end of the world
I am a woman full of rain.
The journey back should be easy;
if this reaches you, wait for me.

—Lisel Mueller, "Letter from the End of the World"

You were once wild here.
Don't let them tame you.

—Isadora Duncan

I learned my name.
I rose up. I remembered it.
Now I could tell my story.
It was different
from the story told about me.

—Eavan Boland, "Mother Ireland"

Marathon of Necessity

She ran, needing to prove herself
a contender in the world
she imagined to be real. The wind
befriended her along lonely miles—
everyone else far behind or ahead.

Sweat in her eyes, she could not see
her destination, only landmarks: a fence,
a dogwood tree, a bed of roses.
Breathless, her body resented
each dehydrating step of this race.

When would she find
victory in her still garden,
the adrenaline adventure of her own pen?
What is enough
is written in the heart's handbook.

Crimson on Plum

What the Bride Wore

A white silk jersey gown,
close-fitting bodice, bouffant skirt
of marquisette. Tulle halo in her hair.

After the honey dropped off the moon—
how Mom told it, winking at Dad—
she accepted synthetics, her closet

a department store paradise lush with
eye-popping shades of yellow and blue,
an occasional red. Mom worshipped

Alfred Dunner, adored his drip-dries.
She even whispered his name
into holy water before Sunday mass.

Silk's fine for the wedding, she said, *but you ought
to have plenty of polyester for the long haul.*

General Custer's Wife

Oh, Autie, we must die together.
—Libbie, in a letter to Custer, 1865

As a young girl she knew loss:
three siblings, her mother.
When she ripened, old grief
emboldened her to reach for glory.
Lovely Libbie Bacon met her dashing *Beau*—
George Armstrong Custer—at a party.
She disliked the gaudy yellow lining of his coat,

yet on their wedding day she carried
roses tied with yellow silk,
the color of his cavalry, the tint
of his long ringlets in morning sun.
On the eve of her marriage, she wrote
every man is so ordinary
beside my own flaming star.

Their wedding an aromatic affair—Libbie
wore orange blossoms in her hair;
the boy general scented
his curls with cinnamon. For weeks
each bore the other's perfume.
Even their eyes aligned: his deep sapphire,
hers the light gray-blue of Lake Erie.

Libbie dared to be her partner's mirror.
She understood his talent for battle, often
risked it all to join him at the front.
My darling sunbeam, my rosebud,
he called her—one letter neared
eighty pages. She answered *my own*
dear Autie, my glorious warrior.

The Sioux made her a widow
at Little Bighorn. Libbie withdrew
into a dark place, refused at first to go out.
For I am wounded, she said,
and a wounded thing must hide.
For fifty-seven years she defended
her husband's good name, missing

my old fellow with the golden curls.
Autie's letters sustained her.
Libbie read them again and again:
My little one, I am yours
through time and eternity.

Jackie

One journalist called it *plum,*
the wool suit Jackie wore
in Dallas. Everyone else said *pink.*

Plum, its sad ending dies on our lips
like a requiem, while *pink*
bounces to the back of the throat.

Color matters
because that suit belongs to all of us.

Now, the ruined Chanel fabric
hangs in a temperature-controlled vault,
sealed for another hundred years.

Eternal couture, worn by a woman
who sat next to her man in the open car—
waving until our future blew up,

became a crimson stain on her skirt,
crimson on plum.

Where Did the Wild Girl Go

in memory of Elaine B. McCarthy

Cityscapes, portraits, nudes
dizzy with vibrant strokes,
flashes of fuchsia, indigo, gold.
Discovery sizzles in this house,
quiet after her sudden death.

Her four children wonder:
Where did the wild girl go?
the one who made such brilliant art
packed away for sixty years
like relics in her attic.

Elaine chose a path inside a frame.
Wife, mother, keeper of the home,
chauffeur and cook—she embraced
her domestic canvas. Later creations
reflect her life, measured, more subdued.
Bowls of fruit, daffodils in pale hues
grace the papered walls.

Her children cheer her on:
Paint your dazzling, gemstone heaven.
Take wing. Be wild again.

Consolation

My mother consoled me with cocoa
the time I didn't win a Girl Scout badge
for the dinosaur I built from a plastic kit,
half the pieces missing.
Maybe I left them
at Rita Knipper's pajama party.
The creature tilted to one side,
a skeleton with two ribs and a tail
that curled like a pig's.
Cold winter nights in upstate New York
my mom and I snuggled under the pink quilt,
concocting stories about Dr. Rex
and the Tyrannosaurus Rehabilitation Center.

Now, my mother hobbles toward ninety,
her fractured hip pinned together
with metal accessories from a surgeon's kit.
In the hospital I watch the way
she tilts to one side,
her legs so white and thin.
Better call Dr. Rex, my mother smiles.
She earned her badge, it gleams
in the space that melts between us.
In that moment I want only to comfort her,
wrap her in a thousand shades of pink.

Girl in a Pink Dress

after *A Quick Nap*, oil on canvas,
Walter Henry Williams, 1952
Baltimore Museum of Art

Gritty traffic sounds pummel summer air.
Still, the child dreams on a tenement balcony.

Powered by pink against her brown skin,
she transforms metal railings into a magic rug

flying far above the fields of real
on gold winds fragrant as vanilla snow,

her cotton candy frock a peppermint
cloud confection. When night falls,

stars shoot past—gilded ornaments
resplendent against the metallic sky.

At a tea party for the angel crowd
she plays pin-the-tail-on-the-moon.

Watch out for that silly cow jumping overhead.
Soon it will rain giant drops of milk.

As first light dawns ballerina pink, she returns
to her rusted home on shimmer-dusted wings.

The Secret Life of Body Parts

After my gallbladder bit the dust
I feared cremation, a digestive dump site.

Where has my uterus gone—is there
a womb hole, a sacred gynecological space?

As long as I picture my ovaries
on a playground, or jiving

at a dance club—a pair of swingers still—
I don't miss them so much.

And what of my friend's left breast?
A pink rose shimmering on a pedestal,

a show-stopping sculpture
below the protective sky.

Because if what is removed
from our earth-worn bodies

finds the light of a safe new home,
I can live with that.

Aunt Emma, On Forgiving the Cow

Uncle Lyman talked funny, his voice
a raspy breath. A white cotton square
covered the hole in his throat.
Too bad the Big C got him, I overheard
family members say. Since Lyman owned

a dairy farm in Pennsylvania,
my nine-year-old mind reasoned
one of those tender-faced creatures
must be the *Big C*. I could not guess
which cow had rendered him silent.

True, Uncle Lyman wasn't mute,
yet each word emerged at a cost,
his face red with effort.
The placid animals looked innocent,
munching grass in dew-speckled fields.

On my summer visit, Aunt Emma
took me into the milking barn. I howled,
sure a beast would attack my neck, destroy
my girly speech. No wonder
that nursery rhyme cow jumped over the moon—

desperate to elude its cruel past.
Nothing to fear, honey, Emma soothed.
Her firm hand caressed each animal's head.
Stunning how she forgave whichever
surly cow had damaged her mate.

Long after the mystery cleared,
when the *Big C* claimed a close friend,
Aunt Emma's strength restored me.
I recalled her gentle, brown eyes, her smile
a calm blessing in country air.

Alice in China

I awake to a Chinese vision on the wall
in the treatment room after acupuncture:
mountains, mist, a rope bridge

straddling a smudge of stream, and a tree
shaped like the porcelain lamp
on the table by my grandmother's bed.

Grandma Alice gave me a kaleidoscope
for my fifth birthday,
forever embellishing my view of the world.

I'm not surprised when a carefree Alice
shows up in this painting, where green
falls from the sky in luminous drops.

On the delicate bridge she calls out—
her voice a cascade, a peppermint cheer,
as she frees her hair from its no-fuss bun

and leaps,
her housedress a blue jewel
vibrant in the crystal stream.

Water splashes onto my forehead;
color returns to my cheeks.

The Body Washer

I wash the bodies of the dead
with water, soap, perfume—
in the name of Allah.
Like my mother and grandmother
before me, I wash only women.
At dawn they bring in the old ones
who died in the night.
By midday, young bodies
stain the stretchers.
Often, so much that is gone.

I do the best I can with what is left.
Since the war, my bloodshot eyes
forget to blink.
I wash each body seven times,
then braid the hair

and wrap the body in a shroud.
Over and over, the same
ceremony brings me peace.
If I falter, who will take my place?
At home, before sleep

I bathe my own daughter,
touch and smooth each flawless limb.

What the Terrorists Do Not See

Esther Nora Gibson, 1962-1998,
Sunday school teacher and oldest of 11 children
—from an obituary in a Dublin newspaper

Later, the mother drew comfort
steeping those moments in her mind:
morning light on Esther's face,
her perfect complexion aglow,
on the way to Omagh
to buy her wedding pearls.

They had lingered over lukewarm
cups of Irish breakfast tea
in the sun-soaked garden where roses leaned
against the wrought iron bench.
Mama, you know I'll find peach beads
the color of my favorite dawn.

In town, the car bomb explodes
a short distance from the shops.
Night reveals a fragment of moon—
a shard of glass pinned to the sky.

Song of Lavender

No visit home this Christmas season,
as carols proclaim Santa's sleigh fest.
Wouldn't you know, I end up
in an ambulance at the ER? Gallbladder
out. Travel plans scrapped. So, I wrap
myself in lavender, an afghan
my mother made, heavy with the familiar
scent of flowers she tied in my curls
years earlier when I stayed home from school
with measles, my face a mess,
my hair a triumphant purple garden.

The afghan quiets my scars, becomes
a coat of blossom. Angels sing
on the radio. I hear my mother's voice.

Glitz at the Musée

Birthday Apocalypse.
Think I'll escape,
reappear in Paris in the Twenties,

wearing only stiletto heels
and lingerie into the Louvre.

A guard will smile, warn me
not to touch anything.

He won't see me fluff my curls
with lavender oil from Provence,
or snap my scarlet garter

behind the bust
of one old pompous duke.

Modern Torso of Apollo

Sibley's Department Store boasted
intricate ceilings, ornate cash registers,
a pride of manufactured male bodies.
High school, I worked part-time
in men's underwear, pajamas, ties.

New stock arrived each week. My job:
undress the headless plastic gents,
reclothe them in the latest styles.
For bikini briefs my boss made me
use the dreaded mini mannequins.

Picture chest to upper leg—a shark
attack minus the gore. I would lean
backwards clutching my half-man,
remove his old undies, and with a swivel
or two, pull on the updated duds.

I became adept at handling torsos.
Romance came later. In the cool hours
before the store opened, when no one
was looking, I would grab a fiberglass
paramour, move like a dancer in heat

across polished floors—dreaming
of proms, chance encounters. Someday
soon I'd meet a guy with a face,
plus all his body parts. He'd talk back
to me, change his clothes daily,
take off his own underwear, then mine.

All of Us Wanted to Be Annette

Dressed up in flannel and slipper socks
at Rita Knipper's pajama parties, we drank pop,
plucked our eyebrows, made ourselves
beautiful. Rita—my best friend—invented
a facial mousse with stuff from her kitchen:
tomato paste, mashed cucumbers,
maraschino cherry juice, Muenster cheese.
Roberta added sprinkles of cinnamon
and pepper to freshen our pores.

By seventh grade we moved to hair. I cut off
six inches of Rita's thick curls,
leaving a bald spot near the top of her scalp.
It's all good, she said, then
trimmed my bangs until my forehead
sported a row of dark blonde teeth.
Glued to the Knippers' black-and-white TV,
we watched *The Mickey Mouse Club*
with Annette Funicello, the star Mouseketeer

glowing in a turtleneck and pleated skirt,
her abundant hair a wild gift.
Years later—body wasted, speech gone—
she died of MS. In a daze,
I rented old Beach Party movies,
hummed "Pineapple Princess," teased my curls.
Annette, you walked in beauty.
Your hair is still a vision.

Charade

I find the hat at Vera's Antique Shop,
where floors slope gently toward Peru.
Morning light caresses
azure bottles on a ledge. A dusty cat
naps atop a rose velour chair.

Posing in vintage leopard and delicate
pearl earrings, I channel Audrey Hepburn
playing detective, my white
Givenchy gloves covered with clues.
I feel fearless in rhinestones, a silk

vanilla-scented scarf—
my faux fur pillbox perched
like a halo on my curls. Am I innocent,
or do I pine for Cary Grant
scintillating in that charcoal-blue suit?

The Language of Hair

Spoleto rests like an elegant hat,
an ancient accessory atop an Umbrian hill.
I studied poetry in that fortressed town,
sequestered in an old stone convent
where nuns lived in silence.

Early mornings I'd walk barefoot
down a long hallway to the bath, dressed
in my leopard pajama shorts, matching top.
Once in a while I'd pass by a nun—
her wimpled head lowered—one eye

lifted to take in the leopard, my sacred garb.
My ex-Catholic face still upbeat
after sixteen years of pious lather.
The bathroom thrilled with its ornate tub, yet
no place to wash my hair. So, twice a week

I risked a beauty salon where stylists
spoke only Italian. I relied on
elaborate gestures, facial antics:
wash blow dry big hair no cut oh please no cut
The ladies laughed, vibrant voices

fueled by espresso, an excess of church bells.
We shared the language of hair, our smiles
an instant translation. Rich shampoos
rendered me radiant. I became
a Roman goddess, a blonde with poems

tucked in bounteous curls—my sonnets
a lyrical spritz. That palace of mousse
remains a postcard in my mind:
black porcelain sinks, towels thicker than
a nun's habit. I entrusted my scalp,

my head, my hair to those *sante donne*—
holy women. Their hands taught me faith,
a touch more nurturing than prayer. Each time
they baptized me, I was a happy babe
reborn in their miraculous suds.

I Shop with the Queen

in memory of Queen Elizabeth II

We primp in a mirror, try on a bouquet of hats
in a millinery boutique east of the palace.
The queen looks smashing in blue, piquant in pink.

Quite formal at first, she loosens up
as we banter about the value of veils.
I like to be seen, insists my famous friend.

Hence, I rarely cover my face,
and my coats and hats always match.
I whisper, *Your Majesty, no one says "hence."*

She smiles serenely, pokes me in the ribs.
We pause for tea in porcelain cups. I ask
if it's grueling to be regal, forever

minding your p's and your q's.
Q stands for queen, she quips,
her posture perfect in gilded light.

P's for pomp, or else for play. With that,
Her Royal Highness commands:
Hand me the fuchsia cloche with plumes.

A Solace of Lilacs

Unveiled

Easter, a solemn procession graces
Our Lady of Good Counsel Church.
All the fourth-grade girls in white
dresses, veils, patent leather shoes,
walk slowly up the incensed aisle.
Each of us carries a lily, long-stemmed.

My lily wanders, somehow snags
the veil of the classmate before me—
Maureen Taramino—whips it off her head.
The motion upsets her hairdo, knocks
her turquoise glasses askew. Her veil
weaves like a drunken sinner

high on the tip of my rogue flower.
The congregation responds with repressed
giggles at first, then a litany of laughter.
I spot Mrs. Nowicki crossing herself twice.
Maureen Taramino bursts into tears. Her mom
casts me a damning glare. Sister Miriam

yanks me out of line, her face beet red.
You did that on purpose, she seethes, forgetting
our limited lily rehearsal time.
She makes me kneel on a wooden pew,
do penance—thirty Hail Marys, head bowed—
while the good girls continue on their holy way.

I sneak a peek at the statue of Jesus,
his Sacred Heart ablaze. He gazes downward
toward the underworld where doubtless
I am doomed to spend Eternity. I vow
to follow a path without veils. My lily
a wilted bloom next to my polished shoes.

Alvina and the Bishop

Aunt Alvina mixed liquids, counted pills.
From St. Mary's basement pharmacy
she sent capsules and elixirs—
small gifts to heal the sick.

Alvina Josephine nurtured patients
she never met, except the Irish bishop
who asked for her, saying
You put the roses back in my cheeks.
He praised her skills in a verse
she kept next to her rosary.

When Alvina's beloved mother died,
Bishop Kearney offered the mass, his brogue
a salve, a consoling prescription,
a present returned to sender.

Spring Break

Damn ninety, Aunt Alvina laments, squeezing
excess skin that hangs from her upper arms.

Pictures from her youth show a shapely girl,
svelte in summer shorts, ruffled lace blouses.
Arm talk resurrects college, my senior year.
Auntie treats me to spring break, a promising week
in the Virgin Islands. One catch: the gift
includes her presence. My friends grin, console
my tainted trip. At the pink-walled Indies House,

a brand-new hotel on a hill in St. Thomas,
we bask for hours in tropical sun. Aunt Alvina
entertains our pool mates with tales of her travels
as a pharmacy rep, starring in drugstore
photo ads across the USA. Waiters listen,
serve us exotic drinks in lime-green cups.
Auntie covers up in straw hats and long sleeves.

Tank tops expose my arms. My glamorous tan
peels, leaving funereal piles of flaky skin.
I resemble a leper; a nurse applies first aid.
The hotel owners choose Aunt Alvina to pose
for promotional post cards, assuring her fame.
She turns them down. *Together or bust,* she toasts
our bond, pats my heavily salved limbs.

Remember the glory days at Indies House,
I remind Auntie now, my arm linked in hers.

Only Trouble Is, Gee Whiz

All I Have to Do Is Dream—Everly Brothers

In my plaid-happy, pre-teen summers I earned
extra coins cleaning my parents' bedroom.

Rows of dust bunnies gathered
weekly beneath the mahogany bed.

Armed with citrus Pledge and polishing cloths,
I listened to my turquoise transistor radio

as the Everly Brothers sang *Dream*
in perfect harmony. I pretended to be

a femme fatale romancing boys
with pompadour hair, frilly shirts.

Their smiles, their cloud-white teeth,
shone in my mind's make-believe suite

like my parents' freshly wiped mirrors.
I remember the ardent scent of lemon,

windows open to our backyard,
to Mrs. Nowicki's intoxicating lilacs.

Afternoon sun reflected off my thick glasses.
In my dream, I could see without them.

Great Elixirs

My dad called them *goo*—
magical serums and ointments
lined up on tall, mirrored shelves
at Siller's Pharmacy on Thurston Road.
Just out of reach,

those potions with power to erase
my adolescent acne, make me beautiful.
I longed to pour all the contents into a porcelain bowl,
dip my face in, emerge a princess, smooth-skinned.
Even the cost of one cosmetic

exceeded my monthly allowance. I wept
in that perfumed emporium. My dermatologist
prescribed an odd-smelling beige astringent.
Liquimat stung my blemishes, rendered me anemic.
I slathered it on my forehead and cheeks

before pajama parties, tried not to envy
Susan Lincoln's pink complexion,
Peggy Atwell's perfect features.
I prayed for a miracle at Sunday mass,
lit white candles, felt the weight of the cross.

Defying my faith, I found hope in fiction.
Charles Dickens saved me. His words—if not goo,
a glue sealing together the lost parts of myself.
On the way home from the library, I passed by Siller's.
Sunlight shone on pricey lotions.

I placed my trust in what came free:
the healing comfort of books.

Pennies from Heaven

On a visit home I arrive at dusk,
a solace of lilacs in our front yard,
the moon a pale copper light.

Stretching my legs in the long driveway,
I enter the house where Mom waits,
her bright face so welcoming.

She sends me back out for Russian tea
and extra pennies. At the Leaf & Bean
I tell the lady behind me in line

my ninety-five-year-old mother
has challenged me to blackjack.
We always play for money, I say.

To my surprise she opens her wallet,
offers pennies. More hands in the caravan
spill a cascade of copper coins.

Mom and I play cards for hours
on her yellow crescent sofa
while the full moon watches over us.

Never mind her own waning body,
Mom defies the odds. That night she wins
thirty-nine games out of fifty.

My Sister's Schizophrenia

I remember her eyes,
sweet milk chocolate alive with light,
a double brilliance: bold sun
on morning water.

In museums I prefer Monet faces,
liquid eyes relaxing into pastel.
I feel safe in their company
where light remains constant.

Some fool repainted my sister's eyes,
took away the light.
Monet would not forgive
this loss of color.

Let This Be the Place

Sometimes I hear my sister call to me
as if she were not far away. Last night in a dream
she helped me search for my lost iPhone,
which doesn't make sense because she died
long before I owned one. *Take everything
out of your purse*, she insisted.

She succumbed at sixty-three to a myriad
of diseases stemming from her mental illness.
This is not a poem about dying
in a pillowed room filled with family and friends.
Nancy passed away in an ambulance, alone
except for EMTs. I got the call at 5 am.

We walk in Sherwood Gardens. My sister laughs,
says we should count all the tulips, at least the reds.
She is holding the toy mandolin she played
as a child. Her voice sounds healthy and light.
Let this be the place her breath runs out.
Let me be with her this time.

You Are Not Alone

something in the girl is wakening
something in the girl is falling
deeper and deeper asleep
—Lucille Clifton, "begin here"

Breonna Taylor, *Say My Name*
you and I shared the same birthday, June 5. Geminis.
Wish we could have raised twin toasts. *Not Gon' Cry*

Did someone say a life nests in small moments? *Broken Wings*
Breonna, "Bre," I want to tell your story—how you loved your job
in health care, playing Skip-Bo and other card games with your
aunts. *Girl, I'm Gonna Miss You*
Music from the 80's and 90's put a sparkle in your step. *Didn't We
Almost Have It All*
Your Aunt Tahasha called you "cool, a cool cat."
"Definitely a diva," confides Tamika—your beloved Mom. *Sweet
Child O' Mine*

You died March 13, 2020, in Louisville, Kentucky.
A reckless police raid. *Nobody's Supposed To Be Here*
Age 26. Black. Shot 6 times.

12:40 am. 3 white officers. 32 bullets fired.
30 minutes after the shooting, *If I Could Turn Back Time*
EMTs checked your pulse. No pulse.

A sliver of solace, Breonna.

Possibly, in the hours before you were slaughtered, *Every Breath You Take*

you lost yourself in the healing magic of song.

Don't You Forget About Me

Playlist (You Are Not Alone)

You Are Not Alone —Michael Jackson

Say My Name —Destiny's Child

Not Gon' Cry —Mary J. Blige

Broken Wings —Mr. Mister

Girl, I'm Gonna Miss You —Milli Vanilli

Didn't We Almost Have It All —Whitney Houston

Sweet Child O'Mine —Guns 'N Roses

Nobody's Supposed To Be Here —Deborah Cox

If I Could Turn Back Time —Cher

Every Breath You Take —The Police

Don't You Forget About Me —Simple Minds

Wendy Darling

I shall sew it on for you, my little man

Wendy's adolescence felt wanting,
until a strange boy without a shadow
flew to her open window.

A helpless stalk of green,
Peter needed more than fairy dust.
He pleaded for a domestic solution.

Instinct traveled to her fingertips.
Thimbleless, Wendy sewed
without a pattern in winter light.

Shadow-task done,
the final stitch filled her hollow spaces.

Boston Marathon, 2013

A blast. Screams.
Smoke and glass.
Her foot gone.

Just one day before,
Adrianne Haslet-Davis
had painted her toes
a promising shade of pink.

They rush her off
without the limb that moved her
through every intricate dance:

> heel first
> toe back
> glide, swivel, skip
> slow-quick-quick.

No time for farewells.
Now, a tourniquet speaks
for the ordinary dress-shoe moments—

a burst of music,
her footsteps light
on the safe and steady ballroom floor.

Elegy for Sandra Bland

July 13, 2015
Hempstead, Texas

Born fragile, like the rest
of us, you make your own way,
struggle to gain a foothold.

Along the path stumbles
and accolades. Your arms reveal
bracelet scars. You persevere,

speak out for justice,
earn a college degree, secure
a job in the South.

Close to making a difference,
only days from a fresh start.
Sandra, your longing so palpable.

A minor traffic stop ends it all—
an escalation, an arrest.
Instead of furnishing a new life,

you find yourself in a jail cell
alone with an intercom.
What monstrous fears darken your mind?

Do you see salvation in a trash can
liner, a way to extinguish
the voices of the dream-crushers?

Possibly, you hum "Strange Fruit."
Oh world, you whisper,
something's gotta change.

Of Mice and Smoke

Bonnie Lynn Fields, 1944-2012

Bette Davis exhaled female allure.
Twin trails of smoke emerged from her nostrils
whenever she pouted or flirted or fumed.
Ingrid Bergman, Lana Turner—they all puffed—
strong dolls with glamorous lacquered nails
holding aloft paper tubes of tobacco.
Silk gowns, fur stoles, tiny rhinestone waists,
nicotine stashed inside chic beaded bags.

Fresh-faced and agile, Bonnie Lynn Fields
danced into the Mickey Mouse Club at twelve,
her breath invested in tap and ballet—
television fame a starburst
glittering her adolescence. Who knows
where she picked up her first cigarette?
Maybe at a pajama party with a pack of friends,
each daring the others to inhale

in sophisticated siren style, á la Bette,
á la Ingrid and Lana.
Bonnie, for years you succumbed
to the lure of Lucky Strikes—
removing the cellophane a ritual
like unwrapping a shiny gift.
On the mantel your Mouseketeer ears,
small dead animals gathering dust.

I Am Marilyn Monroe's Lipstick

Kiss Kiss Red in a brassy tube
upright in her rose-perfumed bungalow
next to rows of rainbow-hued pills.
Even if I could speak, I'd keep
her secrets, the way her hand trembles
as she holds me close to the mirror,
eyes half-shut, mouth an alluring oval.
She never bothers to blot my excess. I am

an enigma, a glossy magnet catching men,
yet part of an arsenal shielding her face
from the animal world: creams, false
lashes, pearly blue shadows, goo. Mascara,
her lacquered sword. How seamlessly
we all play together, guarding our goddess—
the portal to her complex inner realm.

Stashed inside her gold mesh purse
before a long evening out, I know
she will use me over and over,
wear me down, leave my raunchy imprint
on macho flesh. O night of beasts!

Alone in the small hours, she washes me off.
Without my crimson luster—just Norma Jeane.

Marilyn Speaks

My career took shape
in Bed Bath & Blonde.

Men used my hourglass
body to keep time.

Reporters always said
I gave up diamonds

for Lent. In my jeweled
clutch: red lipstick, pink pills.

Makeup concealed
the real Norma Jeane.

Tell me, what more
did you want to see?

My star burned,
set fire to the gold lamé.

Fame killed me, honey.
Before I went down

even my pubic hair
glowed in the dark.

Annie O

Phoebe Ann Moses, born poor
in Darke County, Ohio, 1860.
Before she turns one, her father
freezes to death in a blizzard.
Soon she is sent to live
with a cruel family she calls *the wolves*.
Sharpened by grief, she becomes
a hunter—by fifteen a master shot.

She weds a marksman, Frank Butler,
joins his act. Meets Buffalo Bill Cody,
auditions for his Wild West Show.
Known as Annie Oakley, she thrills
the plains with her gun—shoots ashes
off the tip of her husband's cigarette.
This star attracts another celebrity fan:
Chief Sitting Bull. She lifts his spirits.
He gives her the nickname *Little Sure Shot,*
pays good money for a photograph
of the two of them together.

Oh, Annie, you thrive on fame.
You mesmerize men: Frank, Buffalo Bill,
the Chief—even the Prince of Wales.
Beyond the cymbal sounds of glory
a whisper of sadness in your eyes.
In evening light, do you imagine
trading a portion of your wild life
for a few quiet years with your dad?

Forever Marylyn

Ninety and petite,
a charmer in a celery-green suit,
Marylyn poses at her grandson's wedding reception
near rows of mini cherry pies. She smiles
like a proud mama who has just given birth
to these pastry babies.
Beyond baking, her skilled hands create
patchwork colors, embroidered designs.
On a tour of her Ohio home, I notice scraps of fabric

peppering the front room,
a line of pins up the arm of a chair.
Piles of quilts fill every table and alcove space.
Marylyn Heffelfinger, domestic genius,
exudes old-fashioned country roots. Plain-spoken,
at ease with a sewing machine and oven mitts.

Next stop: Marylyn's bedroom. I expect
a display of family photographs in solid frames,
maybe a sturdy cabinet overflowing with figurines.
Nothing prepares me for Lana Turner's boudoir.
A gilded dressing table mirror reflects shapely
glass bottles offering a whiff of glamour.
Did I miss clues in the scarlet pies, the ornate quilts?
Marilyn glows as I recite the alluring perfume names:
Forever Krystle, Scoundrel, Night Musk, Masquerade.

Madam Seamstress

Hand-painted flowers wilt on the faded top.
The pants need more than a miracle—
sad cloth worn thin in the caboose.

I take my favorite two-piece purple
outfit to June, the petite lady who performs
alterations in my neighborhood.

Madam Seamstress greets me, her face
compassionate—voice ethereal as starsong.
She's known as a sewing needle genius.

Please, can you do something? I plead,
June's merciful touch on my arm an omen.
Time   to   let   go, she draws out the words.

My fists clutch the orchid fabric
on the short ramble home. I mourn
these garments I must pack away

in my sequin-studded-satin
fairy-dusted-make-believe valise,
enfolding the lost remnants of my past.

Yum Yum Gardens

The nickname of my first apartment,
a dwelling akin to Paradise
according to the landlord, whose breath
reeked of mint and Eden.

I shared waterfront views with wild-haired Judy
and her porcupine tattoos, Bernardo—
a Viet Nam vet who never wore a shirt—
Wing Commander Craven,
generous for loaning out his extra plunger,

Charlotte Sinatra, a dowager with a past.
Almost forgot Charlie, handyman
supreme; he always answered *not so good,*
but thanks for asking, if questions arose.

On Saturday nights, ear to the vent, I listened
as my landlord, Jack, a serial Romeo
in the downstairs unit, told every date
all I want is a woman to love.
Each rejection meant a threat to raise the rent.

I woke up most mornings to pleasing noise:
oyster boats heading out to the Chesapeake,
skippers calling to one another—buoyant sounds
carried off by the breeze—half-words

inviting like the smell of bacon
from a small café on Sunday. Those phrases
still warm the dream-heavy hour before dawn—
yum yum syllables I can't quite fathom,
yet they fill net after welcoming net.

Trash Bag Rose

My mother crafted a good luck
black cat from a plastic trash bag
in her Silver Seniors art class.
She called it Rose.

Rose starred as the Halloween
mascot for my speech therapy kids.
Vowels and consonants tricked them.
Yet, they mastered the dramatic *meow:*

high-pitched, screechy, out-of-tune.
Nine lives later, Rose collapsed—
her Styrofoam parts fatally dented
by an excess of affection.

With solemn honors,
the school custodian carried our feline off
to an unseen burial place. Grieving,
I picture Mom adding the snazzy

orange ribbons, pipe cleaner whiskers,
the tail with wiry attitude.
Trash Bag Rose, Wild Mom—you two
feisty babes still conjure magic spells.
You spark an abundance of pluck.

Hope is the thing with salt & pepper shakers

In high school, I teased my best friend
Rita Knipper about her pink tulle bedroom
filled with frills. The centerpiece—a hot,
pink hope chest at the end of her canopy bed.
The hand-painted box held rhinestone bling
napkin rings, lacy tablecloths, small

appliances. I spotted a toaster, the slats
wide enough for a poppyseed bagel.
I could not fathom why Rita
blew her allowance on future domestic bliss.
I forfeited my slim funds at the local
movie theater, eager to immerse myself

in horror films. How could I resist
Blood Bath, Cosmic Monsters, Curse of the Fly?
I failed to muster any thrills for a whisk,
cork coasters, whimsical salt shakers.
While Rita practiced making
marmalade muffins in her kitchen, I fed

my imagination with amputated hands
terrorizing orphans on a misty moor.
Graduation Day, Rita's folks
gave her a gift card for Sears. Her braces
glowed. Her hope chest overflowed.
My parents handed me cash, enough to spend

that whole summer at the RKO Palace,
content to go steady with Boris Karloff,
Vincent Price. I dreamed of a creaky coffin
at the foot of my bed. Inside, a corpse
prematurely felled by a metal mixing bowl—
the stained Sears price tag still attached.

The Sisterhood of the Troubling Parts

My anniversary gleams like a shimmery fish
on my calendar's stream of dates.
March 9th marks twenty-five years
since Dr. Martin Benson sliced me open,
removed one damaged uterus, two
blackened ovaries. *I hate the incision*, I said.
Be glad it's not on your forehead, he consoled.

After I returned home from the hospital
I tossed my tampons, Kotex, plus all other
period paraphernalia. I felt free, an ex-
victim of the monthly scourge. Forget Advil,
bloating, mood swings, bleeding through.
That summer I flew to the Grand Canyon
on a solo menopause trek. I dolled up

in a crimson silk dress at El Tovar,
a South Rim restaurant with ravishing
views of my favorite wonder. I watched
as the sun set in stunning shades of scarlet,
marveled over the layered bands of red rock,
patted my tummy, my own illustrious canyon.
How did I toast my newly lightened pelvic cavity?

I sipped a Campari spritz: mystic
red liqueur—bitter, spicy, sweet.

Wild Raspberry

The History of Female Evolution: A Brief

Small breasts win praise in ancient Rome.
Women wear linen, bandeau-style bras.

In the Middle Ages, wealthy ladies play coy,
their bracelets and unseen garters a match.

The Renaissance favors a pushed-up bust,
wide hips. Leave it to the 16th century:

a sage creates farthingales to highlight illusion—
tightly cinched waists the ideal silhouette.

While men dabble in dirty verbal skirmishes,
frilly silk corsets constrict women, hold in

more than flesh. Cholera damns the 1850's,
overshadows the onset of crinoline.

Skip to the 1940's. Bullet bras shoot toward fame.
Pin-up dames proliferate. Underwear

everywhere. Black-seamed stockings, sequined
bustiers steam up the fashion scene.

Women unclasp their own grievances in the hot 60's,
burn bras, speak up in smoke and lace.

Wild girls continue to blaze,
a sultry blend of Spanx and spark.

Fresh headlines boast
a chorus of gold bodices—

Wonder Women unrestricted, bold.

Beneath the Pomp of Circumstance

after *Dorothea Berck, Wife of Joseph Coymans,*
 oil on canvas, Frans Hals, 1644, Baltimore Museum of
Art

Dorothea, I know you crave fuchsia,
a gown with spaghetti straps,
glitter butterflies above each breast,

mauve on your lips and lids. I see
in your eyes the desire to lighten,
take off that stiff white cape

pinching your neck, those cuffs
like arm restraints. You toss
your missing glove at the artist.

Wipe your brush with this, you call
as you plot the next garment
you'll remove, something heavy and black.

Three and a half centuries you wait
for me to coax you free.
Let me drape you in a whisper of feathers,

cheer as you leave your frame—buoyant,
no one left to judge your dress.
We will primp in a gilded mirror.

When the guard scolds us, let's giggle,
girlfriend, and take him out to lunch.

The Cone Sisters

The Yellow Dress, oil on canvas, Henri Matisse, 1929-31
The Cone Collection, Baltimore Museum of Art

Oh, Etta and Claribel, you gave me *The Yellow Dress,*
        part of my own wardrobe now.

In the presence of shimmer,
        must I wear a burdensome winter coat?

I picture myself slipping
        into glorious yellow taffeta.

Rich spinsters, two sisters,
        Dr. Claribel and Miss Etta Cone

met Monsieur Matisse in Montmartre.
        Art patrons, they lapped up his work.

My Baltimore ladies, he called them,
        his voice steeped in affection.

Austere in long dresses and high Victorian collars,
        early twentieth-century apparel—the sisters

gathered the greatest collection of Matisse
        in the world. On a map, a mere sliver from my home.

A guard spins me around this museum room,
    across shiny, patterned floors.

Everywhere I look,
    a galaxy of light.

Yellow Anthem

The Yellow Dress, Henri Matisse, oil on canvas, 1929-31

—Baltimore Museum of Art

Suppose Matisse grows restless in heaven.
    Too much pastel.

Suppose he hurries back to earth
    sloshing buckets of gold.

Suppose he visits the designer, Miuccia Prada.
    She praises *The Yellow Dress.* They collaborate on a yellow
    coat.

Suppose a young poet dazzles in this garment of hope
    at the Inauguration of a new era.

Suppose we bask in the beauty of Amanda Gorman,
    a star aglow, an exclamation in yellow.

Suppose she paints words we long to absorb:
    For there is always light.

Suppose Matisse smiles in blinding sunshine,
    at home in the passionate language of the world.

Jezebel

Why, when I'm stuck in traffic
on this Maryland highway
rank with billboards,
do I envision myself in a rickety wagon
alongside Henry Fonda—
near death from yellow fever—
riding to a leper colony
in 1850's New Orleans?

Present desperations always
conjure a scene from some old movie.
When atonement seems appropriate,
I welcome Bette Davis.
She appears in a bubble, her sins
upstaged by the noble tilt of her chin.
I lift mine a little higher,

gaze into the rear-view mirror
beyond my red scarf— at a hundred
slow-moving cars. As if on cue
it starts to rain; I chose the worst route.
And I wore the wrong dress to the ball,
Bette sighs. We both sigh. I free
my right hand to place a cloth, a cool
wet cloth, on Henry's burning forehead.

A Sugar Maple Tree on St. Paul Street

after a photograph by Bill Hughes

Every tree needs a red dress
in autumn, a crisp fire-red
fashion statement at November's Ball,
a party in country fields
fueled by apples, cold cider in cups.

Every woman needs at least
one drop-dead red dress, sensual
fabric as much as color
luring her into sin. Even the hem

caught in a fever too quick
to quench. That crimson frock
slinks toward the midnight hour,
bold enough to act on its own.

Stories spring from backless satin,
the daring bodice, a glam of sequins
bawdy beneath the scarlet mystery moon.
Praise the dress. Red. Remember red.

Carnival Blossoms

Leprechaun vibes lure me to Main Street
in the wee town of Limerick, Maine.
A shamrock sign boasts *Lucky Find*.

Georgiana, part pixie, fills her shop to the brim.
Who needs the pot of gold? A gilded dresser
displays bars of soap wrapped in glitzy

paper, or tucked inside rhinestone boxes
lined with tissue. Tahitian Orange, Mango,
and Jasmine compete for scent attention,

until I inhale Wild Raspberry, a show-stopper soap
arousing instant delirium. I'm swooning
as this jam perfume tantalizes—summons

a carnival of blossoms, an amusement ride
spinning me toward paradise. Across the aisle,
rings dazzle. I glimpse a bauble of green glass.

The ring fits. I must be royal, an emerald
princess rejuvenated in this aromatic palace,
ready to rally the frazzled world.

Wild Bill's Wife

Agnes Lake tamed lions. In Abilene,
she met a man with a mane—
his tawny-colored moustache
a long rope above his sensuous mouth.

Tightrope walker, equestrian,
queen of the circus ring—she held her own,
as Wild Bill Hickok in buckskins
spun his Colt Revolvers.

Agnes lassoed him; they wed in Wyoming
in 1876, honeymooned in Cincinnati
for two weeks. Oh, the double sin—
they dropped all finery for flesh.

Five months later, bad news about Bill
from the Badlands. The Pistoleer Prince
shot dead in Deadwood, South Dakota,
during a hot game of poker.

Wild Bill had conquered Indians,
outlaws, buffaloes, bears, yet
tender letters reached his spouse:
Agnes, Darling, if such should be

we never meet again,
while firing my last shot
I will gently breathe
the name of my wife—

Agnes relived the still hours
tangled in Wild Bill's hair,
how she tamed his fears, her murmurs
calming the roar of six-shooters
always sounding in his ear.

Dinner Date with Richard Gere

Wouldn't you know I am wearing
my Donna Karan pajamas size twelve
shrunk to a size eight after two washes?
Late for my dreamy rendezvous—I'd spent
hours curling my lashes, no time to dress—
I grab my faux leopard coat from the closet

even though it's mid-July, the sun
a lemon bruise in a brutal hot sky
and my Toyota Corolla won't start,
so I hail a bumper-stickered taxi
with a driver who speaks only Portuguese.
He heads the wrong way; I guess he assumes

everyone in leopard goes to the airport.
With the help of a Portuguese interpreter
dropped onto the roof of the taxicab
I arrive at last at *Chez Pierre*,
rush toward my Richard, fling open my coat
to greet the source of my feverish joy.

A sibilant exhale escapes
from Richard's lips—those little
sausages I long to suck. Shucks,
he's staring at my pajamas. I never shaved
my legs. No earrings—bartered them
for taxi fare. Richard is walking away.

Wait. He turns, opens his coat.
He's wearing Donna Karan boxer shorts.
We kiss in a swirl of Cashmere Lustre Mist,
the seductive scent by the designer
who brought us together. Oh Donna,
we feel your presence. We'll name
our wardrobe closets after you.

Survival Guide

The second my Burlesque Jazz DVD
arrives in the mail, I wipe it down,

pop in Sexy Sculpt, throw myself
into Abs and Booty Blast.

Sassy, flirty, fierce—this cardio
workout zaps inhibitions.

No face mask needed, feather boas a plus.
I flaunt sequins, hang shimmery

gold tassels from the ceiling fan.
Racy music titillates. Lace

defines me, keeps the virtual
Cleavage Patrol on alert.

Platform shoes walk the walk.
Quarantining alone is an art.

In hot pink spandex, my inner
vixen spills over. How I savor

the slow pull of a sheer glove
down my newly muscled arms.

I Could've Been *The Godmother*, 1983

Dear Al Pacino,

Your soulful gaze mesmerizes me.
I loved you in *Serpico,*
forgave your sins in *The Godfather.*
How could those huge wounded eyes
sanction death by garrote?

I long for my personal close-up, grab
my chance, see you in a play I do not fathom,
can't focus or hear for the bliss.
Near the Kennedy Center stage door,
after curtain calls I linger—

the only fan in sight. When you emerge,
I command a volley of coherent praise
to burst forth from my smitten lips. Instead,
I stand mute, ambushed by your eyes,
gunned down by beauty.

I manage to exhale *Hi Al,* which sounds like *Hail,*
a tribute too mild. I might have kissed
your hand, offered gifts, at least
caught the saliva leaking down my chin.
You sign your name on my program,

disappear into a limo—mobster black
The departure of your eyes
brings giant tears to mine. I replay
our moment together, listen to myself
make you an offer you can't refuse.

Highballs

Jim Beam and ginger ale recall
Christmases in upstate New York,
our house ashimmer in poultry heat,
sprays of fake holly rakishly tucked
behind picture frames—Dad's touch.

Mom and Auntie run the kitchen
like gourmet elves in red and green,
their cooking marathons
fortified with festive highballs
stirred in reindeer tumblers.

Mom raises a toast to the turkey,
a bird she bonds with each holiday,
having stitched it up to hold in the stuffing:
You can't take a sewing needle to something
without making a connection.

For His Maryfrances

He built a bluebird sanctuary
on forty acres of his own land,
because once she told him
how a flock of bluebirds flew low
over her clothesline on her moving day.

Retired from water and sewage,
he drives a blue pickup, wears denim,
dreams in blue—although she's gone,
the girl he met in the company coat closet
after the Second World War. Sure,

she'd see *Oklahoma* with him;
they made a date that lasted.
All the words two people spill
over morning eggs, medium luck,
an occasional rose—
the banter over bills and blessings.

Who can fathom
what images the mind retains?
Even now, the color sings
her name outside his window.

Lament for a Cowgirl

In 2009, Charla Nash was attacked
by a chimpanzee that ripped off her face
—Boston Globe

A light blue gauzy veil
stitched to a jaunty straw hat
shields the ruined flesh
where a face once defined you.

Your calm voice forgives
the chimp that changed you.

Two hundred pounds of fury, a giant
brown wrecking ball, a sudden cannibal—
he lunged, obliterated your hands,
your features, your sight.

You wear your real face on the inside
where memory resides. As a girl of seventeen
you joined the rodeo circuit out West.
A spark in your eyes, the will to hold on.

Beyond your wounds you envision
the chance to ride a horse again.
I was a professional cowgirl, you said.
That was my life.

The Day After Your Suicide

in memory of Kay Weinstein

I watch your ocean, tinged with green,
roll in toward the shore
as it has always done.

Why do these quiet rhythms soothe? Why?
The water's surface
a jewel in morning light.

I heard emerald in your laugh,
in your Southern accent
I would mimic in a playful way.

We practiced our profession—
art, we called it—with zest
in cluttered speech rooms.

We filled the mouths of children
with sounds they learned from us.
Miracles in small spaces.

Indoor skies. Azure moments.
You listened well, Kay, your heart
expansive as the Atlantic

rushing always toward heaven
where emerald and azure meet.

GLORIOUS! Ravens Romp in Super Bowl

—*The Baltimore Sun*, January 29, 2001

The headline crows,
a tease in two-inch letters.

I fantasize such a tribute for me,
thirty years to the day a speech therapist
teaching children to watch their faces

in a mirror, the crisp play of consonants
tumbling into vowels in schoolrooms
hidden from the news.

Listen, I rejoice for my padded heroes.
Their loud muscles—throwing, passing,
punting—wow the world.

Will anyone remember
the small motion of a child's mouth
seconds from victory?

It was enough to be the blonde in blue leggings
coaching teeth into position,
a cheerleader who could sweet-talk:

Your tongue touched down just right.
Oh, what a glorious sound.

Grieving in Home Depot

for Norm

A hands-on working man, your tenor voice
thrilled church hymns. For me, you sang
my romance doesn't need a blue lagoon standing by.
Mostly, you spoke the language of Home Depot.

Three months after your death, I search the store
on Defense Highway hoping to find you. I ask
a helpful clerk for tools to cope with loss.
Long ago, you made my heart expand to realms

I could not fathom. I didn't imagine all that room
inside me. Yes, it ended, yet who knows
how love reverberates through space and time,
walls thick as mist? In the paint aisle I spot

sample color cards with names. One says
Lagoon Blue. My vision blurs. I've been here
before. More than once. With you. No moon
in the sky. No hideaway castle rising in Spain.

The Belle of Baltimore

Elizabeth Patterson Bonaparte, 1785-1879

Daughter of a monied merchant,
pretty "Betsy" Patterson dreams
of princes, jewels, gorgeous gowns.
A palm reader tells her she will marry
a man with a famous last name.
At a ball, The Belle of Baltimore
meets Napoleon's younger brother, Jérôme.
A pink Indian cotton dress draws eyes

to her slender waist. The French naval officer
bows, asks for a polka.
Betsy's gold chain becomes entwined
in the braids of his uniform. *You see*, he says,
we are not meant to separate.
Jérôme's black curls shine.
He calls her *my Eliza.* They wed
on Christmas Eve, 1803, the groom

one year older than his bride of eighteen.
At parties, Betsy wears lavish clothes,
gifts from Jérôme. *Lady Eve*, her critics diss.
I am sure, teases friend Aaron Burr,
that I could stuff all her dresses together
in my pocket, and mistake them for
my handkerchiefs. The new wife pays them
no mind. She relishes this limelight.

Napoleon, now Emperor, frowns on the match.
Jérôme and Betsy sail for Lisbon. She trusts
in the fortune-teller's good omens.
Jérôme buys her emerald drop earrings,
rides off to meet his brother in Milan.
Age twenty, pregnant and alone,
Betsy gives birth to her son, Bo.
In Baltimore, she waits for her mate.

Seasons cycle, time a bleak storm.
Napoleon has the marriage annulled.
Jérôme will not come back for her,
not even to see his own son.
Betsy's heart splinters. *Jérôme, Jérôme,*
have you forgotten everything?
She retreats. For therapy, she cooks
deep-fried oysters, shad croquettes.

Betsy travels, immerses herself in fantasy,
finery, masked balls—especially in Paris
where shadows hover over the Seine.
Prince Gorchakov, a Russian diplomat,
dares to come near. One night,
while dancing a saltarello, he whispers to Betsy,
You are better than you want to appear.
Just what are you looking for?

Saltiness and play spark their bond.
They mock the elegant madness around them.
His light penetrates her shell, yet
she does not speak what she longs to express.
Gorchakov leaves for Rome. Betsy journals:
The letters of Prince G are such a treat,
his absence so delicious, I will not lay myself open
to losing this flattering interest by getting close.

She lets him go, wanders for years.
Old wounds suffocate. Betsy dies at ninety-four,
her burial place in Greenmount Cemetery
far from Jérôme, and the Prince who adored her.
I have been alone in life, she had professed,
and I wish to be alone in death.

For the Love of Death

for P.D. James,
grand dame of English crime writers

When my spirits sink, I lose myself
in murder. A body in the Thames
distracts me from petty jolts:
a dead battery, a case of flu,
my personal map blurred in fog.

I crave an English mystery, a corpse
cropping up in the conservatory.
Adam Dalgliesh, poet-detective,
dissects with ease psyches and clues.
Death seems less grim in his presence.

Before I reach the last page
I'm at loose ends, dreading
a return to my mundane dating scene.
On impulse, I commit a magic act,
insert myself into Chapter Eight.

Now, my hero questions me at the murder site.
I drown in his gaze, even though
a proper alibi eludes me.
My face turns herring red.
Am I guilty of self-exposure? He lifts

yards of yellow crime scene tape,
beckons me beneath the canopy—
his free hand a sudden heat on my shoulder.
I close my eyes and surrender, saved
from early onset rigor mortis.

Iron Maiden

Miranda Mason, my nemesis
in eighth grade, insists I must master
the art of ironing the long sleeves on a man's shirt
if I expect to become a wife.

My mother whips up family meals on time.
Dinner appears at five o'clock.
She stuffs a zillion sauce-stained
recipes into a Betty Crocker box.

Every single female classmate I know
aspires to be a bride with a veil
blushing above a bodice of seed pearls.
Miranda practices tossing a lunch-bag

bouquet over her left shoulder. Once,
it lands on Sister Theodore's head.
Age thirteen and prematurely cursed,
I try to duplicate domestic divas.

I burn holes in my dad's button-downs,
turn a pan of scalloped potatoes to ash
while engrossed in a spellbinding book.
I buy seven yards of white tulle netting

at the dry goods store on Thurston Road
to rehearse the wedding march. My brother
steals it for his science project. He gets an A.
Meanwhile, the boy I love—Dennis Shaw—

signs up for the seminary, chooses to marry
God. With immense relief I pull the plug
on my iron, re-cupboard the cooking pots—
return like a prodigal daughter to denim.

My Plain Romance

Well, howdy buckaroos,
he crooned to his cowboy mates
in those black-and-white Western movies.
Gabby Hayes stood for grizzled and gruff,
looked darn sexy in a plaid shirt—a worn hat
crowning his long, matted hair—
one bath a week in a battered tub.

A sidekick you could depend on,
he stirred up dust, knew how to get a laugh.
I picture Gabby the perfect partner,
a guy who speaks plain talk
through his wild beard,
chews off your ear,
makes you feel giddy, *by cracky.*

Together in a chuck wagon,
he shares his plug of tobacco,
drives us into an old-time sunset
that reeks of frontier smoke.
Beneath a swirl of purple sky,
his serenade a prairie tune
in a whiskery, whiskey voice:

Gabby loves this blue-eyed girl
better than his blue-faced mule.

Noah's Wife

She saw it coming, a catastrophe
worse than the awful rains, the flood.
A thousand animals aboard an ark—
in pairs no less—conjured dread:
a preponderance of fur and tusk,
goat odor in close quarters,
hordes of hippopotami, llamas, other critters
demanding stall service.

Her nose declared mutiny
long before she donned a chef's cap
in the ark's well-stocked kitchenette.
Breathing through her mouth, she fed
bleating beasts without complaint,
for Noah treated her right.
During the day he spoke in Bible-talk,
lifted moist eyes toward heaven.

At night, snuggled under a quilt,
her man whispered tender words, made
the heat in her rise.
She loved the way animals converged in him—
one Noah was more than enough.

Queen Kong

After I watch my missing mate
at the top of the Empire State Building,
I pop a Xanax, pound my chest,
cancel my Netflix account.
Part of me seethes. Dumb ape,
gaga for that ditzy bleached blonde

shimmering like a ripe tart,
a harpy in my partner's fist.
I thought he'd run off
with some big-breasted gorilla flirt,
an island princess, one of us. Never
pictured him in New York in chains.

I cheer when he breaks free, until
he climbs that skyscraper
playing a hairy window washer on speed.
Planes zoom in, aim for his head.
Fear changes his eyes, those black pools
I fell for in our courtship days.

We took pleasure swinging together.
From vine to vine, we made a life.
Grief is such a strange animal.
My beast gave me up for a Barbie,
a doll who shaves her legs.
So, what am I, jungle rot?

To Job's Wife

You remain nameless in the Bible,
ten children dead,
your mate afflicted with sores—
although he manages to secure
his own Book and, presumably,
lucrative movie rights.

Speaking of Job, Charlton Heston
handled all the prophet parts.
The moguls push for Robert Downey Jr.,
Owen Wilson, or Brad Pitt.
They would ooze charisma, charm,
even with facial boils.

Your husband's advisors suggest
Reese Witherspoon play you onscreen.
She shined in *Legally Blonde,* the men say,
seemed to grasp the gist of suffering.
You want Cate Blanchett—her agony-eyes;
she could pull off ten more pregnancies
once Job's good life is restored. You insist

a female must take charge.
From the director's chair you order
special effects, a locust choir,
then orchestrate that scene
where God and Satan duke it out
on a dusty street outside a bar at noon.
You hold the camera steady, Woman.

The Rise of Annie Glenn

Sweethearts from an early age, Annie and John
feel safe in each other's space. Their bond,
forged as Ohio kids, strengthens over time.
He excels in science. She blooms
with musical gifts. At their wedding

John's vows sound steady, strong.
Annie's stutter so severe
words like stones weigh down her mouth.

Astronaut John pilots Friendship 7,
becomes the first American to orbit the Earth.
He moves with ease into the spotlight.

Annie waves at the press,
remains mute. Her tongue a rogue muscle
holding back star power.

At fifty-three, she takes flight,
masters fluent speech at Hollins College.
Annie at last found her voice.
She calls John on the phone, such an ordinary task
once impossible. He weeps.

Lady in Green

June 2-5, 2022

in memory of Queen Elizabeth II

With a flick of her wrist, Queen Elizabeth lifts
a marmalade sandwich from her black Launer handbag
during tea at the palace with Paddington Bear.

This cameo role—captured on video—amuses the crowd
gathered to cheer Her Majesty's Platinum Jubilee.
Just as the world frets about her waning health,

the queen proves at 96 she's as fresh as a school lass.
Humor and spirit intact. Her timing, impeccable.
More than ever, we need her to show us

age may slow the body down, yet never dim the wild girl.
The monarch waves—a smiling bloom in emerald green.
Her signature perfume holds court: *Royal Resilience.*

Mermaids in the Basement

I started early—Took my Dog—
And visited the Sea—
The Mermaids in the Basement
Came out to look at me—
Emily Dickinson (656)

We ride the silver-scaled escalator—
Mom, Aunt Alvina, my sister Nancy, me—
down to the depths of Sibley's, our premier
department store in Rochester. Sweltering air
assails us in this lush bargain paradise

where lace pastel brassieres pile up like sand
dollars on the beach. Dim lighting
gives the mannequins an eerie underwater glow—
akin to mermaids without their sequin tails.
We swim around an island of frothy bathing suits.

Auntie vamps in a dressing room,
wagging her make-believe tail in the mirror.
A salesclerk with crustacean features
waves us toward sunglasses spying from a rack.
At the lunch counter we order hot dogs

slathered in mustard, yellow as neon surfboards.
Mothers guard toddlers bobbing in the aisles,
as time sails by. Sleepy after shopping,
we sift through our brightly colored handbags—
and shell out cash before the tide comes in.

Notes

"General Custer's Wife"

George Armstrong Custer was nicknamed "Autie" as a small child because of his mispronunciation of his middle name. His wife, Libbie, called him "Autie" as a term of endearment.

Journal of Libbie Bacon Custer

American Experience PBS Documentary Film, *Custer's Last Stand*

The Custer Story, The Life and Intimate Letters of General George A. Custer and His Wife Elizabeth, ed. by Marguerite Merington, Univ. of Nebraska Press, 1950

A Wounded Thing Must Hide: In Search of Libbie Custer, by Jeremy Poolman, Bloomsbury USA, 2002

"Jackie"

Jacqueline Bouvier Kennedy, 1929-1994, was the wife of the 35th president of the United States, John Fitzgerald Kennedy—assassinated in Dallas, Texas, on November 22, 1963.

"The Body Washer"

Inspired by Rosemary Frisino Toohey's play, *The Body Washer*

"Wendy Darling"

I shall sew it on for you, my little man, Wendy said. *Peter Pan,* James M. Barrie

"Boston Marathon, 2013"

Adrianne Haslet-Davis was an internationally-ranked ballroom dancer when she lost part of her left leg in the bombings. She has become a global advocate for amputee rights.

"Elegy for Sandra Bland"

Sandra Bland was a 28-year-old African-American woman who was found hanged in a jail cell three days after her arrest during a traffic stop.

"Of Mice and Smoke"

American actress and Mouseketeer, Bonnie Lynn Fields, died from throat cancer 11/17/2012. She was 68.

"The Cone Sisters"

Claribel Cone (1864-1929) and Etta Cone (1870-1949). Avid art collectors, world travelers, and socialites during the first part of the 20th Century. Together they gathered one of the best known collections of modern art in the United States, now part of the Baltimore Museum of Art as a separate wing. The 500 works by Matisse in the collection form the largest and most representative group of his art work in the world.

"Jezebel"

In this 1938 romantic drama, Bette Davis portrays a headstrong young woman in the South whose actions – wearing a brazen red dress to a ball – cost her the man she loves (Henry Fonda). At the end of the film, she redeems herself in a selfless act.

"Wild Bill's Wife"

Letter from Wild Bill to Agnes reprinted in *Agnes Lake Hickok: Queen of the Circus, Wife of a Legend,* by Linda A. Fisher and Carrie Bowers, Univ. of Oklahoma Press, 2009

"The Belle of Baltimore"

Wondrous Beauty: The Life and Adventures of Elizabeth Patterson Bonaparte, by Carol Berkin, Alfred A. Knopf, 2014

"The Rise of Annie Glenn"

Annie Glenn, wife of senator/astronaut John Glenn, suffered from a severe stutter. After years of failed therapy treatments, she found a program at Hollins College in the 70's that dramatically improved her speech and transformed her life—The Hollins Communications Research Institute in Roanoke, VA. She became a sought-after public speaker, and a champion for all who stutter. Married to John for 73 years, Annie Glenn died on May 19, 2020 at the age of 100 from complications of COVID-19.

"Lady in Green"

Launer is a luxury brand of British handbags and small leather goods, celebrating 80 years of heritage. Queen Elizabeth owned approximately 200 Launer handbags, and was seldom seen without one.

Her Majesty, Queen Elizabeth II, was born on April 21, 1926, and died on September 8, 2022, at the age of 96. The two poems in this manuscript honoring the Queen: "I Shop with the Queen," and "Lady in Green," are lovingly dedicated to the longest-reigning British monarch, and the longest-reigning female monarch in world history.

Her light and spirit will never dim.

Special Thanks

With heartfelt gratitude to these fellow poets and friends who offered feedback, support, insight, and sometimes wine or chocolate: Emily Buchanan, Anne Canright, Kathie Corcoran, Jane Elkin, Jean Flanagan, Jacintho, Kendra Kopelke, Danka Kosk-Kosicka, Natalie Lobe, Margaret S. Mullins, Lalita Noronha, Tracey O'Rourke, Joseph Reisberg, Jim Taylor, Carol Tell, Anastasia Vassos, The Carrot Top Poets. Sparkles to Grace Cavalieri, Moira Egan and Dean Smith for careful readings and majestic gleanings. Gold nuggets to my teachers for their Great Inspirations: Mark Doty, Stephen Dunn, Peter Murphy, Michael Salcman, Sue Ellen Thompson, JC Todd. A shimmery shout-out to the entire dedicated staff at Apprentice House Press, especially director Kevin Atticks, and the wonderful team assigned to me: development editor Sophie LaBella, managing editor Corrine Moulds, design editor Riley Kamm, and promotion editor Rachel Brooks. A galaxy of gratitude to Dr. Jason Kalirai, astrophysicist, for his spectacular presentations on the wonders of the universe at the Village Learning Place in Baltimore, and for guiding me toward the Hubble images, one of which appears on this cover.

About the Author

Shirley J. Brewer serves as poet-in-residence at Carver Center for the Arts & Technology in Baltimore, MD and has taught poetry workshops to writers of all ages. In addition to poetry, Shirley earned an MBA from the Maryland Bartending Academy. Her award-winning poems garnish *Barrow Street, Comstock Review, Gargoyle, New Verse News, Plainsongs, Poetry East, Slant,* among many other journals and anthologies. Shirley's poetry books include *A Little Breast Music* (2008, Passager Books), *After Words* (2013, Apprentice House), and *Bistro in Another Realm* (2017, Main Street Rag).

She was a January 2020 guest on *The Poet and The Poem* with Grace Cavalieri, Maryland poet laureate, broadcast from the Library of Congress.

A recent Pushcart nominee, Shirley received the first-ever Creativity Award from the University of Baltimore, where she earned her Master's degree in Creative Writing/Publishing Arts in 2005.

Apprentice
House Press
Loyola University Maryland

Apprentice House is the country's only campus-based, student-staffed book publishing company. Directed by professors and industry professionals, it is a nonprofit activity of the Communication Department at Loyola University Maryland.

Using state-of-the-art technology and an experiential learning model of education, Apprentice House publishes books in untraditional ways. This dual responsibility as publishers and educators creates an unprecedented collaborative environment among faculty and students, while teaching tomorrow's editors, designers, and marketers.

Outside of class, progress on book projects is carried forth by the AH Book Publishing Club, a co-curricular campus organization supported by Loyola University Maryland's Office of Student Activities.

Eclectic and provocative, Apprentice House titles intend to entertain as well as spark dialogue on a variety of topics. Financial contributions to sustain the press's work are welcomed. Contributions are tax deductible to the fullest extent allowed by the IRS.

To learn more about Apprentice House books or to obtain submission guidelines, please visit www.apprenticehouse.com.

Apprentice House
Communication Department
Loyola University Maryland
4501 N. Charles Street
Baltimore, MD 21210
410-617-5265
info@apprenticehouse.com
www.apprenticehouse.com

Printed in the USA
CPSIA information can be obtained
at www.ICGtesting.com
JSHW010922081023
49621JS00013B/224